I Know It Is Nonliving

by Sheila Rivera

first step nonfiction

Lerner Publications Company · Minneapolis

How do I know
it is nonliving?

It does not eat.

It does not breathe.

It does not grow.

It does not move
on its own.

A rock is nonliving.

A toy is nonliving.